"In her debut cookbook, Samah Dada brings the fun, warm spirit we've come to love on social media and television to the page. Filled with creative, irresistible recipes, *Dada Eats Love to Cook It* will bring new energy into your kitchen."

—JULIA TURSHEN, bestselling author of *Now & Again* and founder of Equity at the Table (**EATT**)

"Samah's story and food will uplift and inspire. So bright, passionate, and approachable, this cookbook is not just a series of beautiful recipes but a life story that will inspire and encourage anyone who is obsessed with food and looking to make it their career. Samah's food is healthy, happy, and totally welcoming. I love it, and I just know I will be going back to this book over and over again. Congrats, Samah!"

—EDEN GRINSHPAN, author of *Eating Out Loud*

"Samah Dada is a star. Her recipes rock, and her mind-set about cooking is just where you want to be. You will especially love 'eating your vegetables' Samah's way."

—MICHAEL SOLOMONOV, author of *Zahav: A World of Israeli Cooking*

"Plant-based treats never looked so good. Samah makes it easy to take the guilt out of guilty pleasure."

—CAMILA ALVES McCONAUGHEY, founder of Women of Today

DADA eats

RODALE

RODALE BOOKS
NEW YORK

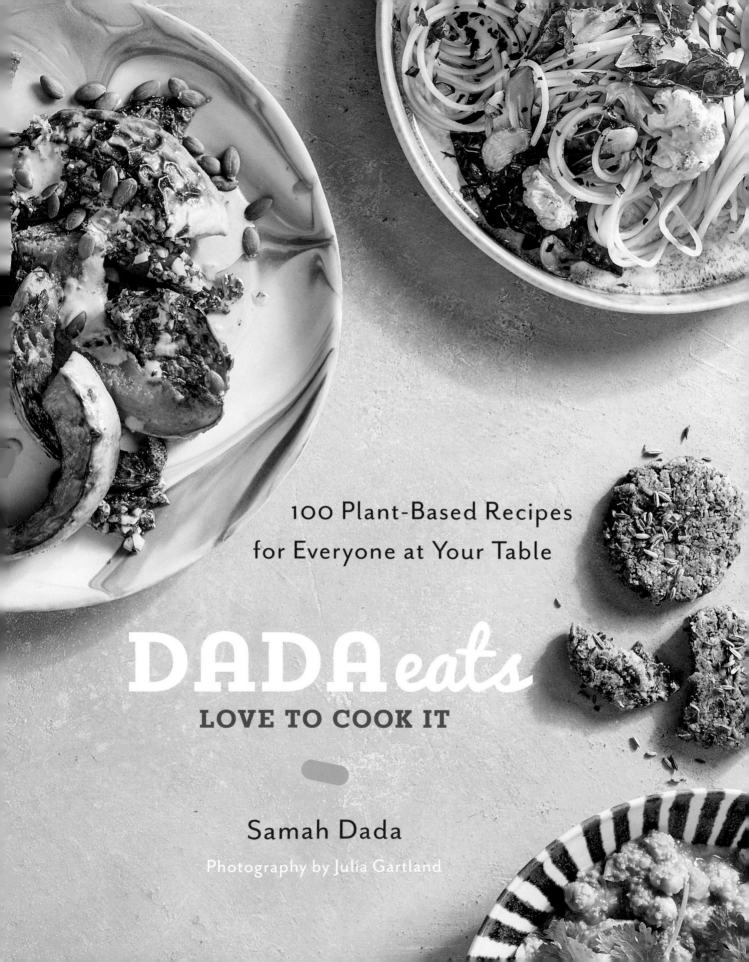

100 Plant-Based Recipes
for Everyone at Your Table

DADA*eats*

LOVE TO COOK IT

Samah Dada

Photography by Julia Gartland

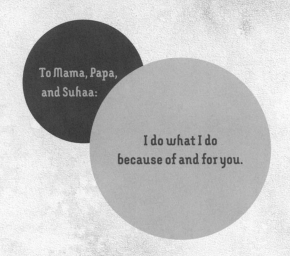

To Mama, Papa,
and Suhaa:

I do what I do
because of and for you.

Contents

INTRODUCTION

How can I adequately sum up what it means to me to be here, sharing with you what is not just my food, but my heart? On one level, food might look like my job. It manifests as a carrot cake with a peanut butter frosting, or hummus so smooth you get emotional. It can disguise itself as tahini used with a heavy hand right to the edge of social acceptability. It is undoubtedly all of these things. But reducing food to just a merging of ingredients would be doing a disservice to myself and to you. For me, food is not simply the end result. It is my hobby that accidentally turned into a career. It is the language I taught myself so I could be better understood. It's how I share myself with others, and ultimately how I became more, well, me.

My parents immigrated to the United States from India when they were in high school, bringing their values and respective parents' recipes with them. Sometimes I wonder how they grappled with raising my sister and me in California after experiencing an upbringing that was so wildly different from ours. Though they instilled cultural values and practices in us both, the reality is that I didn't grow up as part of an Indian community, and as a result, the color of my skin and my Arabic name have constantly made me feel like an aberration.

Though I had friends, it was pretty obvious that I didn't look like the other kids in school, making it even more jarring when I brought *sukha gosht* sandwiches for lunch when my peers whipped out Lunchables and Pop-Tarts. I never felt sure of where I belonged, and my only certainty at the time was that I didn't. I was straddling a line of not being Indian enough, yet ultimately not completely American—and I often still feel that way.

To cope, I became exceptionally skilled at being an accommodating human, friend, and classmate—a perfectionist at being a perfectionist to ensure that, well, if I stuck out, at least it would be in a praiseworthy way. I was, above all, a people-pleaser. And although this innate tendency may have subconsciously given me grief back then by prohibiting myself from failing in any way, I realize now that being wired this way has led me to one of my greatest strengths. It led me to cooking, to pleasing people and their palates. Cooking has become my language for expressing my identity and my confidence in it. Nothing has ever made more sense to me.

I have taken mental notes my entire life, watching my mom cook Indian food every night, wondering if I'd ever be able to comprehend, let alone replicate, the ease with which she'd toss together unmeasured ingredients to yield an unfailingly delicious result. She has taught me so much, yet my path to cooking has materialized as much outside of the kitchen as within it. While a student at the University of California, Berkeley, I assumed the role of unofficial restaurant critic for my friends, always prepared to rattle off a ranked list of my favorite places. Looking for a place to take your parents? Impress a friend? Ethiopian food? The best ice cream? I had everyone and everything covered. I started an obscenely long note on my phone, listing all the restaurants in the Bay Area that I wanted to visit, with asterisks next to them if I had successfully made the trek. I took pride in the street cred my restaurant expertise had bestowed upon me. It was one of the first times in my life that I felt recognized for something that felt like my thing.

It was during college that I became interested in the minutiae of food as it pertained to my well-being. I started taking boxing classes, practicing yoga, and working out at the gym. I also began to pay more attention to ingredients, studied restaurant menus like they were the hottest literature around, and visited the Berkeley Student Food Collective, a nonprofit grocery market dedicated to stocking unique fair-trade health products and local produce. My appetite for information came second only to my appetite for food itself.

After my junior year at college, I moved to New York for a summer internship at CNN, following my dream of working in television. To say I consumed New York voraciously would be a gross understatement. Though my heart knew I'd return to New York again, my brain clearly didn't get the memo. I walked miles to Brooklyn to eat Roberta's pizza, and then a million miles in the opposite direction to get the Salted Crack'd Caramel ice cream at Ample Hills Creamery. I learned the hard way that fresh coconuts from the summer food market Smorgasburg were not worth the price, but definitely worth the photo.

I started running in Central Park, and consequently getting lost in Central Park too many times, almost beginning to enjoy the way my feet hit the pavement. I earned the coveted "local coffee shop," the one where the baristas knowingly smile at you when you swing the door behind you, already prepared to hand over your almond milk au lait, extra hot. I tried vegan sushi for the first time—not the kind with imitation meat, but with ripe mango, avocado, black rice, and a spicy sauce that you want to drown your entire life in. I started checking all of these things off my list, all while watching my phone's camera roll overflow with photos upon photos of food. I decided to put them on Instagram. A part of me thought no one would care, but it wasn't for anyone else but me. My page, @dadaeats, came into existence as a hobby, and I had no intention of it being anything else.

After coming back to Berkeley with more restaurants checked off my list, I dove deeper into conscious eating and intentionally sourced food that made both my body and my soul feel good. At the same time, I ran up against an all-or-nothing mentality. If I care about what I'm putting into my body, am I not supposed to have a chocolate chip cookie? I need cookies to function, and I don't think I'm alone in this sentiment. What about a creamy pasta or chips with queso? Is that not "good"? Who is making these rules? Why are there a million ingredients on the wrapper of this granola bar, and is it just me or do these supposedly "healthy" crackers taste like sawdust? All of these persistent questions and realizations served as the catalyst behind my desire to start developing recipes that sacrificed neither "indulgent" nor "real." If I was disillusioned by the options I found, then I could make my own dishes, simpler ones that used whole ingredients.

After graduating from college and traveling for a month, I ended up moving to New York for my dream job in the NBC Page Program. Armed with my own kitchen for the first time in my life, I discovered that there's a lot you can do in there, even when your arm span takes up the entire width of the kitchen itself. Any way you slice it, the demanding nature of the Page Program should have limited my capacity or desire to cook in my minimal spare hours, but it didn't.

I would go to work six days a week, show tourist groups

around the NBC studios for hours a day, work the *Tonight Show*, and come home to bake brownies. I'd wake up at 3:30 a.m. to get to work at 4 a.m. for my assignment at the *Today* show, change into my stiff Page uniform (you'd love to see it), and head to my wobbly desk in the studio's green-room. I would book cars for our talent and escort guests from their dressing rooms to the set and proceed to come home in the afternoon to immediately blitz spinach and basil in my blender to make a five-minute pesto.

With a new set of best friends in my Page cohort to feed, I had accidentally acquired a second job that I enjoyed just as much as the dream one I had at the network. Beyond that, I became someone in my class who was known for something. I had never felt a sense of belonging like I did in this program. And while that could very well have been because I brought cookies to work every other day, I think it ran deeper than that. Cooking for others without occasion or reason gave me a sense of confidence that finally allowed me to feel seen.

Funnily enough, it was never my aim to make my recipes fall into a specific diet or lifestyle. But a lot of my dishes happen to be vegetarian, vegan, gluten-free, and dairy-free. I don't lead with these labels because they can seem clinical or trendy—I mean, no one is calling broccoli "vegan broccoli." The truth is, by using minimally processed and real ingredients, the results often come with the potential to satisfy a wider audience, including those who battle with dietary restrictions or simply want to follow their preferences.

The accidental plant-based energy of this book, and of my style of cooking, has been just that, an accident—but I couldn't be more thrilled about it. These recipes represent all the ways you can be creative with a short list of ingredients. It's about doing more with less. Sure, I love boasting that the ridiculously soft and chewy cookie you ate was mainly made up of almonds, coconut, and maple syrup. Or that the creamy pasta had no cream in it at all, but was created using just ripe avocados, fresh basil, and olive oil. It can be a flex, definitely, but it's more than that. The fact that my recipes can be relished by individuals who never thought they could enjoy a gluten-free brownie or a slice of dairy-free carrot cake represents the inclusivity that I both chase and seek to shine on every aspect of my work. This is something that I am extremely proud of.

I've noticed that my friends of all ages, those with kids and without, both in real life and on social media, can sometimes feel daunted by the idea of cooking or baking. And even if they love to be in the kitchen, they have busy lives and understandably feel constrained by the limited time they do have to cook for themselves and their loved ones. It's a lot easier to tap a button on your phone and track the journey of your meal on a map than it is to track it from your fridge to a dinner plate. I don't subscribe to everything of the millennial persuasion, but when it comes to food, I get it. Sometimes you want at least near-instant gratification. I mean, you're hungry! You're tired! Maybe you have plans tonight, or this afternoon! Even if those plans are to give your couch some attention with the help of a movie and some popcorn, I know that often the absolute last thing you want to do after a long day at work is to gaze blankly into your fridge waiting for your kale to tell you what to do with it or to stand at your counter, laboriously dicing up onions so fine that you start to cry.

That's the whole idea of this book: recipes that make even the most reluctant and busiest of people want to cook. Whether you're a college student, a young person starting their first job, a mom, a dad, with kids or without, this is where I show you that you can do it. When you want a bright and gorgeous pasta but have only five minutes to make it, I've got you covered with a creamy sauce that you can throw together in your blender. If you just got invited to a potluck and need to bring a dessert and an appetizer, allow me to show you how to skip store-bought hummus and make it quicker (and cheaper) at home, all while whipping up some banana bread muffin tops with that sad and lonely nearly perished banana you have left on your counter from last week. But I also want you to be adventurous, experimenting with spices and recipes that showcase the ingredients I grew up with and the foods I've experienced while living in Europe and traveling to India to visit my family.

Confidence in the kitchen is what has allowed me to exhibit it in every other aspect of my life. It has given me the courage to show off my heritage and the colorful flavors that come with it, instead of hiding it in fear that I won't be accepted. And perhaps most importantly, it has booked me a direct flight to helping people—which is all I ever want to do. Whether it's making your life more fulfilling, tastier, easier, or sweeter, I hope that you'll discover parts of yourself on the pages before you, just as I have. I want you to learn to trust your instincts like I've learned to trust mine. I hope that you will see cooking as a beautiful and messy process, and not as a means to a perfect end result because—plot twist—that perfect result doesn't exist. All it is, is *your* result.

And at the end of the day, I'm not trying to give you recipes that are so complicated you'll flip the page immediately. I want you to look at these little pieces of my heart and soul, use only one bowl to make brownies, and go about your day with plenty of daylight to spare. I revel in the idea of you eating more vegetables than you did before reading this book, because who knew you could even make a tangy, spicy masala with the can of chickpeas hiding in the back of your pantry? I smile at the thought of you telling your friend that you're bringing a lemon olive oil cake to their house, because doesn't that sound chic? It doesn't matter whether you're cooking for one, for two, for kids, or for yourself. We're in it together, and I couldn't be more honored to have you here.

PANTRY ESSENTIALS

Is grocery shopping a hobby? Should I put "expert obsessive grocery shopper" as a skill on my résumé? I'm mildly obsessed with grocery shopping. And when I say mildly, I mean wholeheartedly, absolutely, irrevocably in love with grocery shopping. I find myself in a store at least once a day. I may not even need anything, but you bet walking through those aisles gives me an unparalleled sense of calm and tranquility.

I acquired the grocery shopping gene from my dad, who, like me, also finds strolling through the aisles therapeutic, though I'm sure he'd never admit it. When our family was living in London for a few years, he would frequently make the forty-minute tube trip out to Alperton to visit the many Indian grocery stores there—and would always come home with more spices than we would ever need in one hand and a bag of biryani from a local restaurant in the other.

Even when I'm traveling, I always make it a point to visit a grocery store or four, basically just to see what's up. It's a ritualistic activity that makes me feel a little more at home wherever I am. On the trip home, my carry-on bag is always filled with the fruits of my labor, like crunchy, spicy, savory snacks from India, different types of granola bars and cookies from the UK, or argan oil from Morocco.

When I'm home and operating in my own kitchen, there are some staples you'll never find my pantry without. Tahini, for sauces, dips, and dessert. Nut butters and nuts, for snacking and baking. Legumes and legume-based pastas. Canned crushed tomatoes for pasta sauce and *chana masala*. Some of these ingredients you may already have in your pantry. Some you may need to make a quick trip to the store to buy, or a quick search on the internet to find. Once you have the ingredients listed on the following pages, you can make most everything in this book.

INDIAN SPICES
AND MY SPICE BOX

Growing up, I didn't know of any other way to store spices but in these spice boxes. I'd only ever seen my mom cook with spices that lived in these metal tins, tins that we'd shuttle back from India at the bottom of our suitcases whenever we would make a trip. My mom, and consequently now I, have two separate boxes. One is dedicated to ground spices like turmeric, cayenne, salt, garam masala, coriander, and cumin, while the other is for seeds and other crunchy, sizzling objects of my affection. Think: whole black peppercorns, cumin seeds, fennel seeds, cardamom pods, whole cloves. Even if you don't have these slightly insane spice tins, you can take note of the spices you see inside of them. The ones I use daily are my pantry spice essentials like turmeric, cumin, and cayenne, while others I use more sparingly. Whatever the case, these spices are nice to have around in your kitchen as they amplify flavor and are indispensable in Indian cooking. You can find them at your local grocery store, in international grocery stores, or on the World Wide Web. Make sure you replace your ground spices especially at least every six months (whole spices have a longer shelf life), as spices do lose their aromatics, potency, and flavor over time. If your spices have lost their fragrant smell or don't taste like anything, it's time to say goodbye!

Turmeric

Ground Cumin

Cumin Seeds

Ground Coriander

Cardamom, Cinnamon, Cloves, Whole Black Peppercorns

Mustard Seeds

Cayenne Pepper

CINNAMON

Whether I'm sprinkling it on yogurt, toast with peanut butter and banana, rice cakes, or fruit, cinnamon is a part of my daily routine. Except for when I accidentally mistake my bottle of cumin for cinnamon and start shaking that over my toast. That, I can definitely do without. Cinnamon is a nice addition in pancakes, banana breads, granola, and wherever else you'd like a little kick of spice.

CUMIN // CORIANDER // CAYENNE // TURMERIC // GARAM MASALA

I am grouping these together like a cute little family because these are the spices I grew up with and that will make countless appearances within these pages. Thanks to watching my mom cook with them, I have been accustomed to seeing these spices in her metal spice box, made for heaping up spices and storing them in these ridiculously precious silver bowls. Cumin is one of my favorite spices—I suggest you get both the whole cumin seeds and the ground powder. With coriander, I tend to stick with just the ground powder (and the fresh leaves of course, known as, yep, cilantro!). Cayenne for spice, and turmeric for basically everything else—color, taste, and some gorgeous anti-inflammatory benefits. Garam masala, a quintessential staple in Indian cooking, blends many spices—coriander, cumin, cloves, cinnamon, and cardamom—together. The word *garam* means "heat," though these spices aren't necessarily *spicy*. Rather, in ancient Ayurvedic Indian medicine, they are said to heat up the body and the metabolism.

CURRY LEAVES

Sometimes I think that my mom loves curry leaves more than me. Okay I'm kidding, of course—but they definitely come as a close second. Curry leaves are an irreplaceable feature in any Indian kitchen, and their unique, citrusy flavor and aroma brings life to many dishes. My parents have a plant in their garden, so we feel pretty spoiled, but I do recognize that curry leaves can sometimes be a challenge to track down. You can find them at Indian markets or online either fresh or dried—and if you buy them fresh, you can freeze them to keep for longer. If you're unable to find curry leaves, don't sweat—you can omit in any recipe I call for them. Or you can just come pay a visit to my family's garden, we're happy to share.

SALT

Flaky sea salt is a lifestyle and I am confident that I use it more aggressively than most. Whether it's finishing cookies, pastas, roasted vegetables, my entire life . . . flaky sea salt elevates basically anything you add it to.

Another type of salt I love is pink Himalayan sea salt. This stuff is saltier than the OG and I grind it on top of salads and avocado toast with some pepper and lemon juice on the regular.

And for everything else, I use kosher salt. From seasoning while I'm cooking, adding extra salt to food, to salting pasta water, kosher salt is my go-to.

PASTA

I am super intrigued by alternative-ingredient anythings, so I love a good bean-based pasta. My favorites are chickpea and lentil pastas, however if the bean life is not for you, but you're still in the market for a gluten-free pasta, I also recommend reaching for brown rice or quinoa pasta, which are both delicious, too. When it comes to cooking gluten-free pasta specifically, my main tip is to be a helicopter pasta parent and keep checking it (fish for a piece of pasta and bite into it) until you know it's at your desired consistency. For me, that's al dente. If you leave it in the boiling water for too long, it might get gummy and not hold up. So let's avoid that. And of course it goes without saying that if you are not about the gluten-free pasta life, then choose your favorite type of pasta.

CHICKPEAS

I think I might be chickpeas' number one fan. Whether I'm blending up some hummus, making chana masala, throwing chickpeas in a dessert (please see page 199 if you just raised your eyebrow), or simply pan-frying them in some olive oil and spices so they get golden and crispy, chickpeas are one of my secret weapons. There are so many options of what you can become if you are a chickpea, and for that reason, I always keep a few cans in my pantry. And if I've run out, then someone, anyone, please come find me because something is seriously wrong.

TAHINI

I could probably devote an entire section of this book to tahini (please see my note on it on page 29). At this point it is basically my love language. From salad dressings to cake (yep, that's right), tahini is the savory, grounding flavor you never knew you needed in your pantry. You can typically find tahini next to the nut and seed butters in your local grocery store. If not, the internet is a gorgeous place!

EXTRA-VIRGIN OLIVE OIL

It's worth it to invest in a good bottle of extra-virgin olive oil for a number of reasons. For one, there is a lot of phony extra-virgin olive oil business out there, and often the "extra-virgin" olive oil we see in the stores doesn't actually meet industry EVOO requirements. Yet it can be marketed this way, even if it's diluted with cheaper oils, a bunch of other additives, or chemicals. Good olive oil is different—it should taste fresh, almost grassy, with peppery afternotes. Do some research on the brand of olive oil you're looking at to determine where it's sourced from, and stay away from any olive oil that is kept in a clear bottle. Exposure to light will change the quality of the olive oil for the worse.

CANNED TOMATOES

I'm all for picking up fresh, ripe tomatoes at the store or farmers' market, but it is hard to ignore the convenience that canned crushed tomatoes provide. I use them frequently, if not more than fresh tomatoes, because they are consistent, reliable, and always there for you. Ultimately you can buy them, store them in your pantry, forget about them for a little while, and they'll still be alive. I love to use canned crushed tomatoes for soups, tomato-based pasta sauces, and in Indian dishes like *chana masala* and *baingan bharta*.

ROLLED OATS

When I first started my blog in college, I'd food-style oatmeal like there was no tomorrow. I was like Picasso with those chia seeds. Monet with the berries. Peanut butter was my paint. Flash forward to today, whether it's to make oatmeal, homemade clustery granola, or to blitz in my blender for oat flour, rolled oats are something I always have in my pantry. If you are gluten-intolerant or -sensitive, make sure to buy oats that explicitly say "gluten-free" on the package. While naturally occurring oats are gluten-free, they are sometimes processed in a facility that is not.

HONEY

In addition to being one of my favorite terms of endearment, honey is, in fact, truly my honey. It's a sweetener I turn to for homemade granola and desserts, and even just to drizzle on my daily peanut butter and banana toast. My favorite variety is manuka honey, which is native to New Zealand and sourced from the manuka plant. I love it not just because it has a purer flavor than any other honey I've ever had, but also because it has major antiviral and antibacterial benefits—which for me, makes its higher price point worth it. If you don't have access to manuka honey, I suggest buying honey that only has one ingredient: honey. It's common that some commercial brands will cut their honey products with other sweeteners, which is why I will always recommend local honey if that option is available to you. Additionally, honey won't be as stable in plastic containers, so look to buy it in glass containers when you can.

SEEDS

Chia seeds, hemp seeds, sunflower seeds, sesame seeds, flaxseeds, and pumpkin seeds. These are the seeds I keep in my pantry for snacking, baking, or topping. Seeds add texture, some excitement, and some crunch (what a thrill!), and they are a good way to get in some fiber. We love fiber.

BAKING (AND NO-BAKING)

NUT AND SEED BUTTERS

Peanut, almond, cashew, sunflower seed butter. I cannot emphasize this enough. Nut butter is my life blood. From baking cakes and cookies, to topping rice cakes, to eating with fruit or even a spoon, nut butters are one of those shelf staples that I can't live without. Peanut and almond butter are my two favorites, but I also recommend cashew butter if you prefer a more neutral taste. For my nut-free friends, sunflower seed butter is a great option. If you're baking with it, be warned that the chlorophyll content in sunflower seed butter reacts with baking agents and will cause your cookie or cake to turn green. This is totally harmless and safe to eat. It's mostly hilarious.

JUST SO YOU KNOW

I also recommend keeping a bag of almond meal in your pantry. Almond meal is made from raw, unpeeled almonds, giving it a coarser consistency than almond flour. Almond flour is made from blanched almonds, which lends itself to a much finer consistency, more similar to regular flour. I turn to almond meal for crusts (like in my Spicy Turmeric Quiche, page 75) for a heartier texture.

ALMOND FLOUR

If I can entice you to buy any alternative flour, let it be this one. Almond flour is my absolute favorite to use in the kitchen. Its uncanny ability to make everything taste cakey and moist, dense yet airy, wholesome yet decadent, is one that I've found to be unmatched with any other flour. You'll see it frequently in my desserts because I simply can't get enough of it. It is pricier than regular flour, but remember that the only ingredient is *almonds*, so it also happens to be grain-free and gluten-free. It makes me happy to see that it's widely available in most stores.

COCONUT FLOUR

Coconut flour was maybe wronged in another life because she soaks up three times as much liquid as regular flour. This makes coconut flour kind of a pain to bake with on its own, because it has a pretty high tendency to absorb everything up and leave you with a mildly dry finished product. A little goes a long way! This is why I frequently use it in conjunction with almond flour, because I've found that alongside almond, coconut flour's properties aid in creating a light sponginess that is actually delightful.

MAPLE SYRUP

Taking my pancakes for a swim is just one of the many reasons why I keep maple syrup around. Along with coconut sugar, it's one of my favorite unrefined sweeteners to bake with, and it adds a full-bodied, rich taste to anything it's used in. Maple syrup and pancake syrup, however, are two very different things, with the latter containing a slew of other sketchy ingredients (high-fructose corn syrup, I am looking at you) that I don't love to welcome to the party. Choose pure maple syrup, in the intensity you prefer—whether that's golden (lighter), amber (rich), or dark (robust).

FLAXSEED MEAL

Not all heroes wear capes, and flaxseed meal is definitely one of these capeless heroes. Flaxseed meal is just a more sophisticated term for straight ground-up flaxseed. While flaxseed meal isn't something I'm actively consuming by the spoonful every day (that journey probably would not bode well), it's an amazing kitchen hack to work as an egg replacer when you're baking.

If you're allergic, vegan, or simply have some sort of aversion to eggs, what we call "flax eggs" generally serve as a good replacement. To make a flax egg, combine 1 tablespoon of flaxseed meal with 2½ tablespoons warm water. Set it aside to thicken for about 5 minutes. You should be left with a gelatinous mixture that can be subbed into recipes that call for 1 egg. If a recipe calls for 2 eggs, bump it up to 2 tablespoons flaxseed meal and 5 tablespoons warm water. I've found that using any more than 2 flax eggs tends to compromise the integrity of the recipe as it's written.

NON-DAIRY MILK (ALMOND, CANNED COCONUT, HEMP, OAT, FLAX, I COULD GO ON . . .)

The degree to which the body can process lactose and milk products varies from person to person. What I do stand by is the fact that everyone is just a little bit on the spectrum of lactose intolerance. The good news is that non-dairy milks abound, and it's more a question of what people are *not* milking these days. Cashews, oats, flaxseeds . . . there are a lot of options for non-dairy humans out there. I recommend keeping canned coconut milk (full-fat!) around as well, to make soups and dals, as a substitute for heavy cream in baked goods, and for a no-bake cheesecake filling.

COCONUT SUGAR

Coconut sugar is typically the only type of sugar I keep in my pantry. Also called "coconut palm sugar," it's a natural sugar made from the sap of coconut palms, and is lower in sucrose, making it a good choice for people who are interested in a low glycemic sweetener or just something that's a little better for you than regular cane sugar. While I appreciate the fact that coconut sugar is touted as a better-for-you sugar, that's not the only reason why I use it. My love affair with coconut sugar is due largely in part to the warm, golden taste it brings to baked goods—from cookies to loaf cakes, I lay awake at night thinking about the subtle yet rich sweetness it brings to everything I put it in. In summary, it is something my kitchen and body cannot live without.

COCONUT OIL

Coconut oil is like the friend we all have who's good at everything and it's kind of annoying to watch, but we still love that energy for them. Coconut oil is incredibly versatile—from baking with it, popping popcorn in it, making coconut rice using it, to even lathering your body with it so we can all be moisturized humans, there are no bounds to what coconut oil can do. Note that coconut oil is solid at room temperature and becomes liquid when it has been heated or warmed (a melting point of 78°F to be exact). Many sweet recipes will call for your coconut oil to be melted and then cooled so that it won't coagulate when you're combining it with other ingredients. However, in cases where your coconut oil needs to be "scoopable" but is at a liquid state in its jar, all you have to do is chill it in the fridge, stir it, and then let it rest at room temperature to get it to the consistency you need.

CHOCOLATE CHIPS

Need I say more? Need I? I will anyway. What is life without chocolate chips? Most of the time I even hesitate to note specific amounts for chocolate chips in recipes because we all know that those proportions are rightly measured with the soul. But I humor myself sometimes. There is hardly any more real estate for chocolate in my pantry because I like to stock it with everything: whether that's dark chocolate chips, semisweet chips (some of these are actually dairy-free, so keep your eyes peeled on the ingredients list), bars made purely from 100% cacao, and even some really great sugar-free varieties. I always suggest keeping some of your favorite chocolate bars on hand as well, as these can easily be chopped up for use in any recipe in lieu of chips. And, if you are one of those people who couldn't care less about chocolate, then don't stress, there is still plenty of room for you in this book, too.

CACAO // COCOA POWDER

From brownies to smoothies, cacao and cocoa powder both make many cameos in my place of work. The beans used to make cacao products are raw and in their unprocessed, unroasted form, while in cocoa products, the bean has been roasted at a high temperature and is sometimes cut with other additives or sugar. Cocoa is likely the chocolate taste you're used to—a little sweeter and less bitter than straight up cacao. I typically choose cacao over cocoa because I like that kind of drama and intensity in my life, but they are interchangeable in any recipe you see them in throughout this book. Always reach for unsweetened cocoa powder when baking (we're going to be adding sugar to the recipe anyway!), and check the ingredients to make sure you're only seeing either "cacao" or "cocoa powder" on the list.

RAW CASHEWS

Raw cashews are the ultimate shapeshifter. Because of their lightly sweet, buttery, yet neutral taste, cashews can really be anything that they, or I guess we, want them to be. Soaking cashews in particular softens them and makes them pliable enough to be used in sauces, cheesecake fillings, and dips.

You can either soak cashews overnight in room-temperature water or, if you're impatient like me, you can use the flash-soaking method. This saves us basically . . . a whole night. All you do is boil some water and pour it over the cashews. Let them sit in the hot water off the heat for one to two hours. By the end, they will be soft enough to blend and subsequently transform into whatever you'd like them to be.

Make sure you buy the "raw" variety of cashews—they aren't roasted or salted, and because of this, work well as a neutral base for savory recipes like my Roasted Jalapeño Queso (page 32), or sweet ones like my No-Bake Raspberry Cheesecake (page 207).

RAW ALMONDS

When I was growing up, my mom used to buy raw almonds, soak them in water, and laboriously peel the skin off of each almond for us to eat. I found out later that she did this because our grandma thought that the sweeter, tender taste

TIP

If you've stored your dates in the fridge and they've consequently become a little tough or stale, revive them by boiling some water and pouring it over the dates, allowing them to soak in the water off the heat for 5 to 10 minutes and soften them (but don't leave them soaking for too long as it breaks down the sugars). And if you're looking for an alternative to jam or a sweet spread to have on toast, soak your dates, pit them, and blend them with a little bit of water until a paste is achieved. Add in some vanilla or cinnamon and you have a perfect homemade date spread.

that results from this soaking method would entice us all to eat more almonds. It worked.

In addition to enjoying them as a really reliable snack on their own, I like to transform raw almonds into cheesecake crust, sweet and salty energy bites, and granola. I prefer to buy raw almonds because they're easy to find in bulk and aren't roasted with sketchy oils or additives.

MEDJOOL DATES

There is an extremely high likelihood that by the day's end, I've snacked on a few dates stuffed with peanut butter and finished with some flaky sea salt. Dates are naturally extremely sweet, with caramel and brown sugar undertones that work well whether baked into a dessert (see page 210 for a salted toffee date cake) or simply stuffed with nut butter and coated in chocolate (see page 238). My favorite variety to eat and bake with is the Medjool date, because of its fleshy, chewy texture and unmatchable sweet taste. I always recommend buying the Medjool variety (unpitted) over the more common Deglet Noor dates, as the latter is firmer and drier, making it tougher to work with.

SHREDDED COCONUT AND COCONUT CHIPS, UNSWEETENED

And . . . you thought that there couldn't possibly be another form of coconut in my pantry. Well, look what we have here. Though it probably doesn't cross your mind too often to buy shredded coconut or coconut chips, they are incredibly versatile additions for topping smoothies, adding to homemade granola, or using as a component in baking (and no-baking). Look for the unsweetened kind, as we'll likely be sweetening any recipe we add it to anyway.

Spicy
White Bean
Dip

Tahini
Beet Dip

Any
Occasion
Crackers

(READ: A LOT OF DIPS)

sides
+
apps

Creamy
Sweet
Potato &
Garlic Dip

OG Hummus

Serves 6—8

Hummus is a key component of my personality. Give me your hummus puns, your hummus-centric restaurants, your hummus skepticism (and I'll turn it into adoration). While hummus is traditionally made using dried chickpeas that are soaked and then cooked until they break down, I recognize that canned chickpeas are a lot more accessible and convenient for most of us. I, for one, make hummus using canned chickpeas, and know that this method yields great results. The trick is (1) blending until you literally cannot blend anymore so the tahini and chickpeas really marry each other and become extremely, velvety smooth and (2) not rinsing the chickpeas beforehand so they hang onto the aquafaba (the chickpea brine in the can), which will actually allow for fluffier hummus.

It's also important to pay attention to the tahini. The best, highest-quality sesame seeds are called Humera seeds, and they're sourced from a specific region in Ethiopia. Buy a brand of tahini made with Humera seeds and you're on your way to an obscenely delicious hummus. Whether you're using dried chickpeas or canned, the only thing I urge you to do is to break up with store-bought hummus. Homemade hummus is far fresher and tastier than its store-dwelling counterparts.

¾ cup tahini

Juice of 1 lemon

4 garlic cloves

1 (15.5-ounce) can chickpeas, drained but not rinsed

1 teaspoon ground cumin

¼ teaspoon paprika, plus extra for dusting

Kosher salt to taste

Extra-virgin olive oil for drizzling

Za'atar for dusting

In a food processor or high-speed blender, combine the tahini, lemon juice, and garlic and pulse 4 or 5 times. The mixture will seize and not look too cute at first, but that's normal!

Now add the chickpeas and ¼ cup cold water. Blend until the mixture begins to become smooth.

Now add another 3 to 4 tablespoons of cold water and blend until it is completely smooth. Feel free to add more cold water to reach your desired consistency.

Add the cumin, paprika, and salt. Blend 2 or 3 more times, until the hummus is extremely, velvety smooth.

Season to taste. Transfer the hummus to a bowl, top it with a generous drizzle of olive oil, and dust with paprika and za'atar before serving.

Pesto Hummus

Serves 6—8

When I find a song that I like, I play it on "repeat" until I can't hear it for one second more. I've taken a similar approach to hummus, in that I eat it over and over again, but in this case, I *never* get sick of it. While I hope to grow as a human in general, I really hope that my inherent ability to always hold a space in my soul for hummus is a character trait that is here to stay.

I created this particular recipe in an effort to bring the brightness of pesto to hummus, and the creaminess of hummus to pesto. It's zesty, fresh, and light, and sneaks a ton of greens in without you even registering what's happening (hear that, parents?). Chickpeas, tahini, basil, and spinach are all key players, but don't forget the cumin and smoked paprika. I also live for the act of adding za'atar (a Middle Eastern blend of herbs, commonly oregano, marjoram, cumin, coriander, sesame seeds, and sumac) on top of my hummus—find it on the internet or in the international section at your grocery store.

1 (15.5-ounce) can chickpeas, drained, reserving 1 tablespoon aquafaba (that liquid in the can), but not rinsed

⅓ cup plus 1 tablespoon tahini

3 tablespoons extra-virgin olive oil, plus extra for drizzling

Juice of 1 lemon

3 garlic cloves

⅓ cup (packed) fresh basil leaves

¾ cup (packed) fresh baby spinach

½ teaspoon ground cumin

¼ teaspoon smoked paprika, plus extra for dusting

Kosher salt to taste

Freshly ground black pepper to taste

Za'atar for dusting

In a food processor or high-speed blender, combine the chickpeas with the reserved aquafaba and the tahini, olive oil, lemon juice, garlic, basil, spinach, cumin, and paprika. Blend 3 to 4 times until completely smooth. Season with salt and freshly ground black pepper.

Transfer the hummus to a shallow bowl. Finish with a drizzle of olive oil and garnish with a dusting of za'atar and paprika before serving.

Tahini Beet Dip

Serves 6—8

You're probably wondering, WOW, Samah, are you . . . obsessed with dips? And I can confidently say: YES. Yes, I am obsessed with dips. Do you blame me, though? You can throw everything into a food processor or blender and, with the push of a button, it's done. All of my dip recipes require minimal time and equally minimal ingredients. Yet once you spoon them into a nice bowl and add a garnish, they look so sophisticated and almost like you've spent your entire life in the kitchen making them. And listen, sometimes it really is about less time in the kitchen and more time to enjoy with friends or even just with yourself. A party of one is still a party.

The deep pink color of this dip, created by the beets, objectively makes it pretty, well, pretty to look at. The sweetness from the beets is undercut by the savory tahini, creating a divine depth of flavor. With the addition of lemon and garlic, it's tangy, flavorful, not too sweet, and a little addicting if I'm real with you (and I always will be).

1 cup chopped cooked beets (about 5 baby beets—I often use the vacuum-packed cooked beets in the produce section of the grocery store)

¾ cup tahini

Juice of 1 lemon

3 garlic cloves

1 tablespoon extra-virgin olive oil

¼ teaspoon smoked paprika

Kosher salt to taste

Freshly ground black pepper to taste, plus more for garnish

Flaky sea salt for garnish

Handful of fresh cilantro or parsley leaves, roughly chopped, for garnish

In a high-speed blender or food processor, combine the beets, tahini, lemon juice, garlic, olive oil, paprika, kosher salt, and ground black pepper.

Blend or process on high until completely smooth. You may have to scrape down the sides of your blender to ensure everything is thoroughly combined.

Transfer the dip to a serving bowl and garnish it with sea salt, freshly ground black pepper, and the cilantro.

A NOTE ON TAHINI

I am overwhelmed. Where do I begin? I guess I could start by saying that I have loved tahini for as long as I can remember. Somehow, some way, many people have even told me that I was the one who first introduced them to tahini. I cannot fathom a higher compliment than that.

Though I've eaten tahini for years, I first bought the sesame substance of my dreams to make hummus at home—but let's just say that my foray did not end with hummus. I started baking with tahini, putting it into energy bites, into cookies, and more famously, into my Chocolate Chip Tahini Cake with Chocolate Frosting (page 187), which has become one of the most popular recipes I've ever written.

So what's the deal with tahini, anyway? Tahini, which comes from the Arabic word *tahana* meaning "to grind," is made from sesame seeds that are ground into a paste. It can be made from hulled or unhulled sesame seeds, often toasted to expel a nuttier flavor, and made into a consistency that sort of resembles peanut butter. Sesame seeds have been cultivated in India since 5000 BCE (what's up, ancestors), and today they're grown in many different regions. It's thought that tahini itself originated in what is present-day Iran, but it has since spread throughout the eastern Mediterranean and many other parts of the world.

Tahini is my kitchen's MVPP (Most Valuable Pantry Player). It is one of the ingredients I use the most for its versatility in lending itself well to both taste and texture. In baked goods it undercuts the sugar and balances out the chocolate. The buttery notes make it perfect for cookies or cakes, but equally as great in salad dressings and hummus. I often use it in pasta, or combine it with spices and herbs to make a sauce for roasted vegetables. Tahini is widely available, but it's crucial to look for the ones with minimal oil separation and where the ingredients are just "sesame seeds." The best tahini is made with Humera sesame seeds, which are sourced from a particular region in Ethiopia, so if you can do some research on the brand of tahini you're using, all the better.

Spicy White Bean Dip

Makes about 2½ cups

In my family, going to a restaurant means asking the servers, "Do you have any chili sauce?" This question may vary depending on the type of cuisine; maybe "red pepper flakes?" or simply "anything spicy?" For us, pizza should come with jalapeños, onions, and green peppers—all controversial, questionable toppings that we will always still top with red pepper flakes. Let me be clear, we are never adding chile to stifle the taste of the food itself, but rather to please our very-much-accustomed-to-spicy-Indian-food palates.

As a result, I always like to have a bit of spice in everything—not to the point where you feel like you can't enjoy what you're eating, but enough so that your taste buds are a little surprised and awakened every time you take a bite. This roasted jalapeño dip will not let you down in that department.

1 jalapeño

Extra-virgin olive oil

1 (15.5-ounce) can white beans, drained and rinsed

¾ cup tahini

4 garlic cloves

Juice of 1 lemon

½ teaspoon ground cumin

Kosher salt to taste

Za'atar for dusting

Paprika for dusting

Preheat the oven to 400°F. Place the jalapeño on a small parchment-lined baking sheet and drizzle it with olive oil so that it is nicely and lightly coated all around. Roast in the oven for 10 to 15 minutes, until the skin starts to peel and blacken and the jalapeño becomes tender. Remove the jalapeño from the oven, remove the stem, and set it aside to cool. If you'd like this dip to be less spicy, you can slice the jalapeño open and remove the seeds.

In a food processor or high-speed blender, combine the cooled jalapeño with the beans, tahini, garlic, lemon juice, cumin, and salt. Process or blend until incorporated.

Tablespoon by tablespoon, add cold water until the mixture thins to your desired consistency. I typically use 4 to 5 tablespoons, but I encourage you to use more or less depending on the consistency you like! Blend until the dip is extremely smooth. Season to taste with salt.

Transfer the dip to a bowl. Before serving, drizzle generously with olive oil, and top with a dusting of za'atar and paprika.

Creamy Sweet Potato & Garlic Dip

Serves 6—8

Every day, and this is a fact, I ask myself, how can I consume sweet potatoes today? Should I bake them? Cut them into cute triangles and sauté them with masala? Or should I boil them, and allow the little beta-carotene wonders to start a friendship with tahini, fresh garlic, and spices, for a dip? If a dip calls to you today, then you're in luck. This one pulls in sweetness from the potatoes but is also smooth and savory with the grounding addition of tahini. It's the type of dip that will make you rethink your "sweet-potato-dip-is-only-for-Thanksgiving policy."

2 medium sweet potatoes

¼ cup tahini

3 tablespoons extra-virgin olive oil, plus extra for drizzling

4 garlic cloves, smashed

Juice of 1 lemon

½ teaspoon paprika, plus extra for dusting

¾ teaspoon ground cumin

Kosher salt and freshly ground black pepper to taste

Handful of chopped fresh parsley for garnish

Sesame seeds for garnish

Bring a large pot of water to a rolling boil. Add the sweet potatoes and boil until they are completely soft and cooked through, 20 to 30 minutes. Drain the sweet potatoes and let them cool completely.

Once cooled, peel the sweet potatoes, discard the skins, and place the peeled potatoes in a food processor or high-speed blender. Add the tahini, olive oil, garlic, lemon juice, paprika, cumin, and salt and pepper. Process or blend until completely smooth.

Season the dip to taste. If you want more of a kick, add extra paprika. If you think it needs some more tang, add an extra squeeze of lemon! Make sure that you're both tasting and adjusting the flavor to your liking—at every step of the way! Season to taste with salt and pepper as well. Transfer it to a bowl and drizzle with olive oil. Garnish with the parsley, sesame seeds, and a dash of paprika (aesthetics, we love it).

Roasted Jalapeño Queso

Makes about
1½ cups

I love the idea of creating flavors with ingredients that you don't necessarily think belong at the party. Cashews are probably the last thing you think of when you're craving queso. But the creamy, buttery consistency created by the cashews, the fiery kick from a roasted jalapeño, and the "cheesy" taste thanks to nutritional yeast all work together here to create a velvety, luxurious dip that you may want to bathe in, but should probably just eat with some tortilla chips.

I want to touch on nutritional yeast because while it doesn't have the cutest name, it does work wonders in creating a cheesy flavor, minus the cheese. It is a deactivated yeast, a form of the same strain used to leaven bread, but it's been dried out to extract its gorgeous nutritious benefits. It's really high in B-complex vitamins and other minerals. You can find it in health food stores or in grocery bulk bins. It's also great in popcorn (check it out with my Masala Popcorn on page 242) or on top of avocado toast for a unique savory kick.

1 jalapeño

Extra-virgin olive oil

1 cup raw cashews, soaked overnight or "flash-soaked" (see page 21)

2 garlic cloves, smashed

½ cup nutritional yeast

½ cup vegetable broth, plus extra if needed

Kosher salt and freshly ground black pepper to taste

Tortilla chips or Any Occasion Crackers (page 47; optional)

Preheat the oven to 400°F. Place the jalapeño on a small parchment-lined baking sheet and drizzle it with olive oil so that it is completely coated. Roast the jalapeño in the oven for 10 to 15 minutes, until it is tender and the skin begins to blacken. Remove the baking sheet from the oven, remove the jalapeño's stem, and set the jalapeño aside to cool. For a less spicy queso, slice the jalapeño open and remove the seeds.

Drain the soaked cashews and place them in a high-speed blender or a food processor. Add the garlic, nutritional yeast, vegetable broth, and roasted jalapeño. Blend until the mixture is completely smooth and velvety. I live for a thick queso but if yours is coming out too creamy for your liking, blend in a couple extra splashes of vegetable broth.

Season the queso with salt and pepper to taste, and transfer it to a bowl.

Serve immediately, with tortilla chips or homemade Any Occasion Crackers!

Cucumber Ribbon Kachumber

Serves 1–2

In Indian cuisine, *kachumber* is simply always on the table. It's like that one friend who you can't *not* invite to your party. A medley of diced tomatoes, onions, cucumbers, lemon juice, and often green chiles, kachumber serves as a refreshing complement and palate cleanser to all the deliciously spicy Indian food it is often served with. I decided to take traditional Indian kachumber and instead shave the cucumber into ribbons for some extra glamour. You can do this with a simple vegetable peeler, shaving down on one side of the cucumber until you reach the seeds, then flipping it over to shave the other side. This is perfect as an accompaniment to your mains, or as a great light snack when you need something to keep you and your palate cool and refreshed.

½ red onion, diced

1 cup fresh cilantro leaves and tender stems, roughly chopped, plus extra for garnish

½ cup grape tomatoes, halved

1 green chile, thinly sliced (seeds removed if you don't want it to be too spicy), or ½ to 1 whole jalapeño, thinly sliced

1 large hothouse cucumber, or 5 Persian cucumbers

Juice of 1 lemon

Kosher salt and freshly ground black pepper to taste

In a medium bowl, combine the red onion, cilantro, grape tomatoes, and sliced chile.

Start by peeling the cucumber and discarding the skin. Now, use the vegetable peeler to shave the cucumber until you reach the seeds, rotating the cucumber around to each side so that all you are basically left with is a cucumber-seed carcass. Transfer the cucumber ribbons to the bowl.

Add the lemon juice and season to taste with salt and pepper. Garnish with cilantro. Serve immediately!

Masala Sweet Potatoes

Makes about 2 cups

If you've ever had a *dosa* (a South Indian savory crepe), it was probably served with masala-spiced potatoes, bright yellow in their turmeric glory, with mustard seeds and cilantro. The potatoes practically beg dosa eaters to use the thin, crispy crepe as a vehicle to scoop them all up. The only issue I have with those potatoes is that they often serve as a sidekick, usually hidden inside the dosa itself. They're arguably not essential to dosa consumption and you can order a dosa without, but they come simply as just . . . a welcome addition.

I devised this recipe solely to seek justice for masala potatoes. Dramatic much? Okay, maybe a little bit. Nonetheless, I was inspired by those South Indian–style potatoes to create my own version using sweet potatoes. And they don't need a dosa to shine! They're perfect on their own, as a dish to bring to a potluck, or to eat alongside your favorite savory breakfast.

1 tablespoon extra-virgin olive oil

½ teaspoon mustard seeds

1 small yellow onion, sliced

Kosher salt and freshly ground black pepper to taste

½ teaspoon ground turmeric

½ teaspoon ground cumin

⅛ teaspoon cayenne pepper (you can use ¼ teaspoon if you like it spicier!)

1 sweet potato, cut into small wedges

Handful of fresh cilantro leaves, roughly chopped, for garnish

Heat a medium skillet over medium heat and add the olive oil.

When the olive oil starts to shimmer, add the mustard seeds. After a few seconds, when the mustard seeds start to sizzle, add the onions and cook until they are translucent and starting to brown around the edges, 3 to 5 minutes.

Season the onions with salt, black pepper, and the turmeric, cumin, and cayenne. Cook for a few minutes, until the masala smells aromatic. The "raw" masala smell should have dissipated at this point. Then, add the sweet potatoes.

Cover the skillet and cook over medium heat for 10 to 15 minutes, or until the sweet potatoes are tender, making sure to stir them intermittently. Season with salt to taste. Garnish with the cilantro and serve!

Snacking Bread

Makes 1 loaf,
10—12 slices

Bread is an integral part of Indian cuisine. While many are used to prodding and spearing veggies with a fork, Indians are scooping them up with fluffy naan, some thin golden-brown roti, or a crisp, flaky paratha. I can say with confidence that I was conditioned in my youth to have a deep appreciation for bread in all its forms. It was always there to supplement the food on our table.

Given my history with bread, it felt wrong not to have a go-to recipe in this book. The best part about this one is that it is completely customizable to your taste, whether you want to add garlic and rosemary, some scallions, or keep it simple with sea salt and freshly ground pepper. Go off and get creative; just stick with the ingredients you see here as your base and you'll be well on your way to the bread of your dreams. Note that this is a snacking, shorter stacked bread rather than one that rises higher, allowing it to be fluffy while still remaining perfectly dense, satisfying, and hearty.

2 tablespoons coconut oil, melted and cooled, plus extra for greasing the pan

1¼ cups almond flour

3 tablespoons coconut flour

2 tablespoons psyllium husk powder

2 tablespoons flaxseed meal

2 teaspoons baking powder

1 teaspoon garlic powder

1 teaspoon kosher salt

4 eggs

1 tablespoon apple cider vinegar

Preheat the oven to 350°F. Either grease a 9 × 5-inch loaf pan well with coconut oil or line the bottom and sides with parchment paper and lightly grease the parchment with coconut oil.

In a medium bowl, whisk together the almond flour, coconut flour, psyllium husk powder, flaxseed meal, baking powder, garlic powder, and salt.

In a separate medium bowl, beat the eggs with the apple cider vinegar. Stir the 2 tablespoons coconut oil into the egg mixture.

Combine the wet and dry mixtures and transfer the batter to the prepared loaf pan. Bake for 35 minutes or until the edges are golden brown and start to pull away from the sides of the pan. Cool in the pan completely before enjoying. Slice and store in an airtight container for up to 4 days on the counter, or a week in the fridge!

Hummucado Toast

Serves 2–4

I started making *hummucado* (a word I fully made up, I am aware) toast several years ago, around the peak of the avocado toast craze. At the time, I had yet to see anyone combine my two love languages and slap it on my third love language, so ultimately it was up to me to make my dreams come true. I actively enjoy making this for myself at any time of the day (maybe with a side salad or topped with an egg), but it also makes for a great light bite when you have guests over. So when I'm not smashing some avocado, hummus, lemon, and spices onto a piece of fresh sourdough or my homemade snacking bread to eat myself, I'm slicing this toast up into slivers for my dinner guests to enjoy pre-entrée.

2 slices sourdough bread or your favorite bread

1 avocado, halved and pitted

2 tablespoons hummus (check out page 25 for a homemade option)

1 lemon wedge

Kosher salt

Freshly ground black pepper

Red pepper flakes

Fresh basil, sliced tomatoes, sliced radishes, za'atar, and/or extra-virgin olive oil for garnish

Toast the slices of bread.

Scoop the avocado flesh out of one half and smash it onto one of the slices of toast. Repeat with the remaining half avocado and toast. Then, spread the hummus on top of the smashed avocado.

Squeeze the lemon wedge over the hummus, and season with salt, black pepper, and red pepper flakes.

Garnish the toasts with basil, tomatoes, radishes, za'atar, a drizzle of extra-virgin olive oil, or any additional toppings. The choice is yours!

Turmeric Cornbread

Makes
16 pieces

I didn't discover cornbread until I went to college. Right near the campus, there was a salad and sandwich place called Smart Alec's (that has since closed down! cue single sad tear!) that would bestow a complimentary plate of fries upon you if you brought them a paper that you got an A on. While I don't think that Berkeley students needed the added stress of missed potato opportunities every time a B showed up on their papers, I do know that even better than the fries was the cornbread that arrived as a side with every salad. It was unbelievably buttery and sweet and delicious, and though I told myself I went to Smart Alec's to get the salad, it was really the cornbread I was aiming for. My version here is a turmeric cornbread that uses coconut oil instead of butter and turmeric for spice and color. It is crumbly and light, yet decadent enough to transport me back to the one I fell in love with at Smart Alec's.

1 egg

⅓ cup coconut oil, melted and cooled, plus extra for greasing the pan

1½ tablespoons honey

1 cup unsweetened almond milk

¼ cup coconut sugar

¾ teaspoon ground turmeric

1 cup almond flour

1 cup medium-grind cornmeal

2 teaspoons baking powder

¼ teaspoon kosher salt

Preheat the oven to 400°F and grease a 9-inch round cake pan with coconut oil.

In a medium bowl, beat the egg and then mix it with the coconut oil, honey, almond milk, and coconut sugar. Whisk in the turmeric. Set aside.

In a separate medium bowl, whisk together the almond flour, cornmeal, baking powder, and salt.

Combine the wet and dry ingredients. Transfer the batter to the prepared cake pan.

Bake for 15 to 20 minutes, until the top is golden brown. Let the cornbread cool *completely* in the pan before cutting it into pieces; otherwise it will crumble (though please note, this is supposed to be a crumbly cornbread).

Sweet Potato Aloo Tikki
with Spiced Coconut Yogurt

Serves 4–6

1 medium sweet potato

½ teaspoon garam masala

1 teaspoon ground cumin

½ teaspoon ground turmeric

¼ teaspoon cayenne pepper

Kosher salt to taste

¼ cup plus 1 tablespoon oat flour

1 tablespoon coconut flour

1 tablespoon extra-virgin olive oil, plus 2 to 3 tablespoons for pan-frying

½ teaspoon fennel seeds

½ teaspoon cumin seeds

Handful of fresh cilantro leaves, roughly chopped, for garnish

Flaky salt, for garnish

Spiced Coconut Yogurt

1½ cups coconut yogurt

⅛ teaspoon cayenne pepper

½ teaspoon chaat masala

½ red onion, diced

¼ teaspoon ground cumin

Juice of ½ lemon

Handful of chopped fresh cilantro leaves

Kosher salt and freshly ground black pepper to taste

The culture of street food in India is unlike anything I've seen elsewhere in the world. *Chaat*, as it's called, is the all-encompassing word for Indian street food, which consists of a variety of deliciously crunchy, mostly fried snacks made complete with different chutneys, spices, and vegetables. Chaat is food, but it is much more than that. For Indians, it is truly a lifestyle. This is apparent the second you get a glimpse of the hundreds of food carts found at every corner on the streets of India, serving as a pause for all who sidle up and eat their chaat standing next to the stall. It is an appetizer. It is a full meal. It is a break from life.

In Hindi, *aloo* translates to "potato," and *tikki* to "patty" or "cutlet." These are a recurring pair in Indian chaat, typically deep-fried and served with an amalgam of spices, yogurt, and other crunchy textural elements. My version of aloo tikki uses sweet potatoes and is pan-fried instead of deep-fried. I include all the usual suspects in the spice department, with the addition of olive oil–sizzled cumin and fennel seeds. With a topping of fresh herbs and a side of spiced coconut yogurt, they're my ode to chaat, made to eat at any time of your day.

Bring a small pot of water to a boil, add the sweet potato, and boil until it's completely tender and soft, 20 to 30 minutes. Set it aside to cool for about 10 minutes, and then peel the skin off.

Make the Spiced Coconut Yogurt: In a medium bowl, combine the yogurt with the cayenne, chaat masala, onion, cumin, lemon juice, cilantro, and salt and pepper. Adjust with spices to taste. Mix until fully incorporated. Store in the fridge while you finish preparing the aloo tikki.

Make the Sweet Potato Aloo Tikki: Once the potato has cooled and the skin has been discarded, mash the potatoes using a potato masher or a fork. Add the garam masala, ground cumin, turmeric, cayenne, kosher salt, oat flour, and coconut flour and mix everything together.

Heat the 1 tablespoon olive oil in a small skillet. Once it begins to shimmer, add the fennel and cumin seeds. Let them sizzle for about 1 minute and become fragrant. Now, add these toasty seeds and oil to your mashed sweet potato mixture, and mix to combine. Stir until thoroughly incorporated.

Form the sweet potato mixture into patties using about 2 tablespoons each. Heat a couple tablespoons of olive oil in a skillet and pan-fry the patties until they are golden brown and crisp on each side, 4 to 6 minutes per side on medium-low heat.

Garnish the patties with the chopped cilantro and flaky salt. Serve immediately, and with the Spiced Coconut Yogurt.

Any Occasion Crackers

Serves 4–6

I've always been a huge snacker, especially when it comes to savory goods like popcorn, crackers, and chips. I love a nice crunch and need texture with pretty much everything I eat. I also love eating what I like to call "vehicles," and by this I mean vehicles for toppings like hummus, guacamole, my creamy vegan queso (page 32) . . . you get the point. These Any Occasion Crackers (or as my family likes to call them, "Suhaa's Crackers" because my sister Suhaa can't survive a week without them) really do live up to the name—they're perfect for, yes, any occasion, by themselves or as a vehicle. I find a great amount of joy when adding some za'atar, garlic, and cumin seeds to the flour, or even just keeping it salty and simple with some freshly ground black pepper and sea salt. You could also toss in some oregano and red pepper flakes for a pizza vibe, or nutritional yeast for a cheesy (albeit, cheeseless!) crunch. See more flavor ideas (page 48) and choose your adventure.

Cracker Dough

- 1½ cups blanched almond flour
- 1½ teaspoons garlic powder
- ½ teaspoon ground cumin
- 1 teaspoon salt (I like fine sea salt here)
- Freshly ground black pepper to taste
- Spice mix (see Flavor Options, page 48)
- 1 egg

Egg Wash

- 1 egg
- 1 tablespoon unsweetened almond milk
- Pinch of flaky sea salt, plus extra (optional) for sprinkling

Preheat the oven to 350°F.

Make the cracker dough: In a medium bowl, combine the almond flour, garlic powder, cumin, salt, and black pepper. You can bake as is, with just these spices, or use this base plus your spice mix of choice on page 48. Stir well.

Beat the egg in a small bowl, and add it to the almond flour mixture. The cracker dough will be pretty thick, and feel dry at first, but keep mixing so that everything is well incorporated. It helps to use your hands here to knead it together. After a few minutes of kneading, it should feel like it can stick together.

Place the dough on a piece of parchment paper about the size of a large baking sheet, ensuring that it is on a flat surface. Place another piece of parchment paper on top of the dough, and use a rolling pin or a bottle to roll the dough between the two pieces of parchment. Roll until the cracker dough is spread out and quite thin. (If you'd like thinner crackers, you can divide the dough in half, roll both portions of the dough out super-thin, and bake the crackers in two batches.)

(recipe continues)

Peel the top layer of parchment off the cracker dough. Using a large knife or pastry/ravioli wheel, cut the cracker dough into 1- to 2-inch squares. You don't need to separate each cracker piece, but make sure you've fully cut through the dough so it will be easy to break off into pieces after emerging from a journey in the oven. Transfer the parchment paper with the dough pieces to a baking sheet.

Make your egg wash: In a small bowl, beat the egg, almond milk, and pinch of salt together. Very lightly brush the tops of the crackers with the egg wash. Note that you won't use all of the egg wash—save the rest for your next batch!

Sprinkle the crackers with salt if desired, and place the baking sheet in the oven. Bake for 15 to 20 minutes, rotating the pan halfway through baking, until the crackers are golden brown around the edges. Remove them from the oven and let them cool on the baking sheet completely before breaking them into the pieces. Enjoy with dips or solo! Store in an airtight container on your counter for 4 to 5 days (if they last that long . . .).

FLAVOR ADVENTURES

ZA'ATAR & CUMIN SEEDS
½ teaspoon za'atar +
1 tablespoon cumin seeds

TURMERIC & SPICE
½ teaspoon ground turmeric + ¼ teaspoon cayenne pepper +
½ teaspoon garam masala

PIZZA
1 teaspoon dried oregano +
½ teaspoon red pepper flakes +
½ teaspoon ground cumin

CHILI CHEESE
¼ teaspoon smoked paprika + ¼ teaspoon ground cumin +
1 tablespoon nutritional yeast

ROOTS

My parents came to the United States from India when they were both in high school—my mom to Texas and my dad to Wisconsin. I feel nauseous when I think about that, putting myself in their shoes. Though their lives were marked by Indian traditions, to me, my parents are as American as they are Indian. But because of their own respective upbringings, they've always reminded my sister and me of our culture and where we come from.

While I could not be more proud to be Indian now, I felt self-conscious about it growing up. Even though there were a few other kids of color in my school, I never really felt like I belonged among anyone, infrequently acknowledging my background to my friends for fear that I would be exposed, that they would have true confirmation that I wasn't really like them. It didn't help that every single teacher I've ever had would have to pause before saying my name, internally deciding whether to give it a try or to give up completely, usually opting to scan the room for me, somewhere in the back, with warm pink cheeks, reluctantly preparing to provide some assistance.

I was able to acknowledge my obvious cultural differences during elementary school International Day events, where I'd dress up in traditional garb and offer up some *gulab jamun* (a very, very syrupy-sweet, albeit heavenly, dessert), or *samosas*, to the kids and parents who passed by my stand. I constantly fielded the classic "Where are you from?" question, the one when you know the other person is looking for an answer that isn't "California, like you!" When I celebrated Eid and came to school with henna adorning my hands, I talked about Ramadan and described Eid as, I guess, sort of like your Christmas or Hanukkah?

Feeling othered from young people instilled in me this notion that my worth rested on fitting into the mold. I didn't want to be different. I didn't want to look different. Most kids at that age just want to feel invisible enough, normal enough, to mesh seamlessly with everyone around them. To complicate my feelings even more was the fact that I barely saw anyone who looked like me—not in school, not on TV, not in the books I read. As a kid, I idolized Princess Jasmine from *Aladdin* and dressed up as her for a minimum of four Halloweens because she came the closest to resembling someone I looked like (despite not even being real). And though I felt that I didn't belong in California, I don't fully belong in India, either—I am somewhat of an outsider there as well, speaking less than stellar Urdu with an American accent and exhibiting clear Western mannerisms and clothes. I feel as though I've been caught up in a lifelong balancing act between two cultures each to which I feel tied to strongly, and yet not at all.

Despite all of this, there has always been one place where I felt completely at home with my culture, and that was the dinner table. It made more sense here. The non-negotiable in my family when I was growing up was dinner—and no matter what each of us had going on, we would always sit down at the table together. And I jumped at any excuse to break from my homework to watch and help my mom cook. Everything was methodical but not precise—she, like my grandma, never measured anything before it reached the pot or pan. I have never seen her touch a measuring cup or spoon in my life. At the time, this was baffling to me. She would toss in curry leaves, sprinkle in turmeric, roughly dice a few tomatoes, and somehow—*chana masala, dal saag, biryani*—would all emerge perfectly.

It made no sense. "How can you replicate this if you don't know what you did in the first place?" I'd always ask incredulously. She would always quip that a dish never actually turns out exactly the same each time she makes it. After making something she'll often remark, "Wow, this is actually really good!" as if she's surprised. I never am. From my mother I learned that the key to cooking is to rely mostly on *andaaz*, which in Hindi translates to your own style and estimation. And that, to me, is one of the best parts of cooking—you iterate and change until you surprise even yourself.

Though my mom would cook multiple dishes a night, she was never in the kitchen for hours. She has always had a particular style of Indian cooking; her dishes are a little lighter and brighter, without using any dairy or exorbitant amounts of oil. She would swap cream for fresh tomatoes to change what would normally be a cream-based masala into one that was tomato-based. In a similar way, I have found myself intrigued by alternative ingredients, baking with almond flour instead of all-purpose, using coconut oil instead of butter, challenging myself to create in a way that is different from what is considered the norm but has my own stamp on it. My version, my take.

At the time it never occurred to me that my friends might never have had this type of food, nor this ritualistic dinner experience with their whole family every night—using your hands as utensils, tearing into pieces of roti, scooping up rice, all together. Nearly every night it was my mom's home-cooked food, sometimes pre-gamed by *bhel puri* (my dad's favorite snack).

At the dinner table, I no longer felt the pressure of my cultural balancing act. It didn't matter that Indian people my age were living across the world—they were likely also eating dal and rice with their hands, next to their own siblings and probably all of the aunties, too. It also didn't make a difference that I felt like an outsider in my school and even among my own friends. I felt comfortable here, in this routine of eating as a unit, with intention.

To revel in sitting down at the table across from family instead of the TV was something I learned from my culture and my home. Regardless of where you come from and where you've been brought up, who you are, who you'll become, food has and will always be our common denominator of connection, conversation, and love. I didn't register any of this at the time because I didn't have to. Unlike my place in other aspects of my life, this part just felt right.

Carrot Cake
Muffin Tops

breakfasts to dream about

One Banana Only Muffin Tops

Carrot Cake Muffin Tops

Makes 8—10
muffin tops

When I was in high school and still living under the same roof as my sister, mom, and dad, all four of us would go for morning walks into Newport Beach.

When my dad was feeling indulgent, he would buy his favorite carrot coconut cashew muffin from a café on the way back. He'd wait until we got home, pop it in the toaster to warm it up (there are few things we don't toast), and then finally eat it. These Carrot Cake Muffin Tops are an ode to him.

When it comes to muffins in general, I feel confident that all of us (or at the very least, *most* of us) can agree that we are in the game solely for the tops. There's something about that golden crispness from the caramelization of the sugars (and Maillard reaction!) that, in my opinion, gives muffin tops the lead over their fluffy inside. Since muffin tops are made on a baking sheet rather than in a tin, we maximize the esteemed opportunity for sugar caramelization by allowing heat to hit more surface area of the muffin top. I always gravitate toward making muffin tops for this reason. But it should go without saying that if you're eating muffins just for the inside, I respect your journey, too. *Pictured in chapter opener photo, page 52.*

2 eggs

3 tablespoons coconut oil, softened until scoopable

1 teaspoon vanilla extract

¾ cup coconut sugar, plus extra for topping

1 cup (packed) grated carrots

1 cup almond flour

1 cup oat flour

1 teaspoon baking powder

1 teaspoon ground cinnamon

½ teaspoon ground ginger

¼ teaspoon kosher salt

½ cup unsweetened shredded coconut

Crushed raw, unsalted nuts (optional; I like crushed almonds and pistachios here)

Preheat the oven to 350°F and line a baking sheet with parchment paper.

In a large bowl, beat the eggs. Add the coconut oil, vanilla, and coconut sugar. Mix until completely smooth. Add the carrots to the mixture and stir to combine.

In a separate medium bowl, whisk together the almond flour, oat flour, baking powder, cinnamon, ginger, and salt.

Add the flour mixture to the carrot mixture. Fold to combine so that everything is thoroughly incorporated. Now add the shredded coconut to the muffin batter. You can even add some crushed nuts if you're feeling like you want a little extra texture (and we love texture!). The batter should be fairly wet.

Scoop 3- to 4-tablespoon amounts of the batter onto your lined baking sheet. Sprinkle about 1 teaspoon of coconut sugar over each of the muffin tops.

Bake 25 to 30 minutes, until the edges are crisp and the muffin tops are golden brown.

Let cool slightly on a wire rack before enjoying.

Rice Crispy Granola

Makes
3–4 cups

One of my deepest darkest secrets when making granola at home is to use brown rice crisps in addition to the traditional rolled oats. Not only does it take the crunch factor up intensely, but it also adds a lot more texture and makes the granola simply more interesting to eat. What will I get in this bite? Oats? Rice crisps? Nuts? All of the above? That, in essence, is the multi-layered experience of eating this granola. I like to crush the almonds and cashews slightly so that they catch more of the nut butter and honey—you can do this by placing them in a ziplock bag and hitting them with the bottom of a measuring cup, simultaneously getting out any of your aggression.

⅓ cup creamy almond butter

¼ cup honey (you can sub maple syrup, but I love the way honey works with the rice crisps)

2 tablespoons coconut oil, melted and cooled

1 cup raw almonds and cashews (or raw mixed nuts), slightly crushed

¾ cup unsweetened coconut chips

1 cup rolled oats

1 cup brown rice crisps cereal

1 tablespoon hemp seeds

1 tablespoon chia seeds

1 tablespoon flaxseed meal

½ teaspoon kosher salt

½ teaspoon ground cinnamon

Preheat the oven to 325°F and line a baking sheet with parchment paper.

In a medium bowl, combine the almond butter, honey, and coconut oil, and mix until smooth.

In another medium bowl, combine the nuts, coconut chips, rolled oats, brown rice crisps, hemp seeds, chia seeds, flaxseed, salt, and cinnamon. Add this to the almond butter mixture.

Stir to combine so that all of the dry ingredients are well coated in the almond butter mixture. At this time resist the temptation to snack.

Transfer the granola mixture to your parchment paper–lined baking sheet. Spread it out evenly so that everyone has some personal space and you can ensure an even crispness.

Bake for 30 to 40 minutes, tossing the granola every 10 minutes or so to ensure that everything becomes golden and toasty.

Once you remove the granola from the oven, do not stir it! This is how we achieve clusters (our granola goal), so let the granola sit until it is completely cool before breaking it apart and enjoying. Store in an airtight container or sealed mason jar on your counter or pantry for up to 2 weeks.

One Banana Only Muffin Tops

Makes 4—6 muffin tops

Do you have a lone banana sitting on your counter? Just one? That has maybe been sitting there for a few days, just staring at you, wondering what will become of its existence? Every time I would see one sad banana on my counter, it always served as a reminder that I couldn't whip up a full banana bread, which typically calls for more than one banana. And that realization is the exact reason why this recipe was born. This is the recipe to make if you're craving banana bread but have only one banana to work with.

This is a small-batch recipe, meaning it makes only four to six muffin tops, depending on how large or small you'd like them, which I find to be perfect if I'm just craving a little something sweet at the end of the day or to pair with my morning coffee. I sweeten these with just a touch of maple syrup, which you can totally swap out for honey if that's more your speed. You can omit the chocolate chips if you'd like, but do you like happiness? Then don't skip them. *Pictured in chapter opener photo, page 53.*

1 egg

1 ripe banana

2 tablespoons creamy almond butter or peanut butter

2 tablespoons maple syrup

½ tablespoon coconut oil, melted and cooled

¼ cup almond flour

¼ cup coconut flour

¼ teaspoon baking powder

½ teaspoon baking soda

⅛ teaspoon kosher salt

⅓ cup chocolate chips (I usually measure this with my soul), plus extra for topping

Preheat the oven to 350°F and line a baking sheet with parchment paper.

In a small bowl, beat the egg.

In a medium bowl, mash your one banana. Add the beaten egg, almond butter, maple syrup, and coconut oil and stir the mixture together until it's smooth.

In a separate medium bowl, whisk together the almond flour, coconut flour, baking powder, baking soda, and salt.

Combine the wet and dry ingredients and fold in the chocolate chips.

Scoop 3- to 4-tablespoon amounts of the batter onto your lined baking sheet. Place extra chocolate chips on top, if desired (this is something I always desire).

Bake for 15 to 20 minutes, until the edges are golden brown. Let the muffin tops cool slightly before removing them from the baking sheet. Transfer to a wire rack to cool further before serving or enjoy warm straight out of the oven.

Fluffy Pillow Pancakes

Makes 6–8 pancakes

I basically go to sleep thinking about what I'll eat for breakfast the next morning. And the thought of eating these Fluffy Pillow Pancakes in the morning? Chief among those dreams.

Let me run it back for a second. Once upon a time, I was a pancake mix kind of gal. My family and I used to be all about them. Now, let me be clear—there's absolutely nothing wrong with pancake mixes. But when I realized how simple it is to make a pancake batter from scratch, I was forever changed. (And my alarm clock was also changed. To an hour earlier. So I could eat sooner.)

The name of these Fluffy Pillow Pancakes speaks for itself—they are truly little clouds of heaven, made even more delicious and customizable by the toppings of your choice. I want you to use them as a perfect canvas for anything sweet and extra; choose your add-in adventure below, and top with maple syrup or honey to seal the deal.

¾ cup almond flour

2 tablespoons coconut flour

½ teaspoon baking powder

⅛ teaspoon kosher salt

Dash of ground cinnamon to taste

2 eggs

2 tablespoons coconut sugar

½ teaspoon vanilla extract

½ cup almond milk

Optional add-ins of choice (below)

Coconut oil, for greasing the skillet

Maple syrup, honey, or other topping of choice

In a large bowl, whisk together the almond and coconut flours, baking powder, salt, and cinnamon.

In a separate medium bowl, beat the eggs, then stir in the coconut sugar, vanilla, and almond milk.

Combine the wet and dry ingredients, mixing well. Fold in your choice of add-ins (or leave the batter as is).

Grease a large skillet with coconut oil and set it over medium heat. Spoon 2- to 3-tablespoon amounts of the batter onto the hot skillet. Let the pancakes cook until the edges start to curl up and the pancakes become golden and fluffy, 3 to 5 minutes. Then flip them over and cook until the other side is golden, another 3 to 5 minutes.

To serve, top the pancakes with maple syrup, honey, or your choice of toppings. (I like fresh berries, nuts, cinnamon, and coconut flakes.)

CHOOSE YOUR ADVENTURE:

BANANA
Mash half a ripe banana and fold it into the pancake batter until thoroughly incorporated. Slice the other half of the banana into coins and sauté them in ½ tablespoon coconut oil over medium heat until golden brown on both sides, 3 to 5 minutes per side. Serve on top of the banana pancakes.

BLUEBERRY
Stir ⅓ cup fresh or frozen blueberries into the pancake batter.

CHOCOLATE CHIP
Stir ¼ cup mini chocolate chips into the pancake batter.

The OG Green Smoothie

Serves 1

Green smoothies are obviously not a novelty. There is a lot of "green smoothie noise" out there, in the sense that everyone has a version that they like to make. This is mine.

I have been making this combination for years, and even people who aren't into green smoothies like it. Because, first of all, it doesn't taste green. Oh, and you just *know* when something tastes green. Grass is something I prefer to look at rather than taste, thank you very much. (And maybe not even look at it for too long. I'm mildly allergic to grass.) Make sure your bananas and spinach are both frozen, as this will help to create a thicker, creamier smoothie—a watery smoothie is not cute. We don't want to wake up to that.

1 or 2 frozen bananas (see Note)

½ cup frozen spinach

1 cup unsweetened almond milk

1 tablespoon chia seeds, plus (optional) extra for garnish

1 tablespoon almond butter or peanut butter, creamy or crunchy, plus (optional) extra for garnish

1 teaspoon cacao nibs (optional)

¼ teaspoon vanilla extract

Dash of ground cinnamon

Granola, homemade (page 55) or store-bought, for garnish (optional)

To make the smoothie, combine the bananas, spinach, almond milk, chia seeds, nut butter, cacao nibs (if using), vanilla, and cinnamon in a blender. Blend it up!

If you want to make a thicker smoothie bowl, add 1 more frozen banana and use just enough almond milk for the smoothie to blend. Garnish the smoothie or bowl with your favorite toppings—I turn to granola, more chia seeds, and more nut butter (always).

NOTE

Freeze your ripe bananas by removing the peel, slicing, and storing the chunks in a reusable container or bag in your freezer!

Peanut Butter & Jelly Smoothie

Serves 1

I spent at least eight years of my youth eating a peanut butter and jelly sandwich every day. It would appear that for me, the PB&J transcended its personality as a cute, easy, kid-friendly school lunch to become, well, an inherent part of *my* personality. It felt only right to transform this iconic combo into a smoothie. The frozen banana works here as the sweet and creamy base, and I like to add both blueberries and strawberries as the "jelly." Feel free to use all blueberries or all strawberries if that feels more true to your jelly journey. It goes without saying that you don't need to be shy with the peanut butter here, it's probably why we're all on this page in the first place.

1 or 2 frozen bananas (see Note, opposite)

1 cup unsweetened almond milk, or more to taste

½ cup frozen blueberries

⅓ cup frozen strawberries, plus (optional) extra for garnish

½ cup frozen spinach (optional)

2 tablespoons peanut butter, creamy or crunchy, plus (optional) extra for garnish

½ tablespoon chia seeds

½ tablespoon cacao powder or unsweetened cocoa powder

Chopped roasted peanuts (optional)

Granola, homemade (page 55) or store-bought, for garnish (optional)

In a blender, combine the banana, almond milk, blueberries and strawberries, spinach (if using), peanut butter, chia seeds, and cacao powder. If you want a more drinkable versus spoonable consistency, add a little more almond milk. Blend it up!

If you want to make a thicker smoothie bowl, add 1 more frozen banana and use just enough almond milk for the smoothie to blend. Top the smoothie or bowl with your toppings of choice—in this smoothie I like to add roasted peanuts, granola, and strawberries.

Pancake Bread

Makes 1 loaf,
10—12 slices

Imagine. Imagine a world in which you can eat pancakes in a bread form with a sweet and golden cinnamon sugar topping. Well, all I have to say is that it's a good thing that you're here because this is a world in which you can now live.

If you want a good laugh, just envision me sitting on the floor of my sub-500-square-foot apartment in New York, thinking about all the ways in which I can make pancakes happen in other forms. I'm thrilled to announce that this pancake bread is a product of that thought spiral. It's somehow perfect for breakfast with a drizzle of maple syrup, but also makes complete logical sense as a dessert or midday sweet treat. I put it here, alongside my breakfast staples, because there's really nothing better than knowing you have another form of pancake to guide you out of bed in the morning.

Batter

- ⅓ cup coconut oil, melted and cooled, plus extra for greasing the pan
- 2 eggs, beaten
- ⅓ cup maple syrup
- 1 teaspoon vanilla extract
- ½ cup full-fat coconut milk
- ⅔ cup coconut sugar
- 1¼ cups oat flour
- 1¼ cups almond flour
- ½ teaspoon baking soda
- ½ teaspoon baking powder
- ⅛ teaspoon kosher salt
- ¼ teaspoon ground cinnamon

Cinnamon Sugar Topping

- ⅓ cup coconut oil, softened
- ¼ cup coconut sugar
- 1 cup oat flour
- ½ teaspoon ground cinnamon

Preheat the oven to 350°F and grease a 9 × 5-inch loaf pan well with coconut oil.

Make the batter: In a medium bowl, mix together the eggs, ⅓ cup coconut oil, maple syrup, vanilla, and coconut milk until smooth.

Add in the coconut sugar and mix until everything is well incorporated.

In a separate medium bowl, whisk together the oat flour, almond flour, baking soda, baking powder, salt, and cinnamon.

Combine the wet and dry ingredients, mixing well. Transfer the pancake bread batter to the prepared loaf pan, tapping the pan on the counter and smoothing out the top to make sure it is even.

Make the Cinnamon Sugar Topping: In a small bowl, combine the coconut oil, coconut sugar, oat flour, and cinnamon. Sprinkle the cinnamon sugar topping over the batter in the loaf pan.

Bake for 15 minutes. Then reduce the heat to 325°F and bake for an additional 30 to 35 minutes, until the edges of the loaf are nice and golden brown, and a knife inserted in the center comes out clean.

Let cool completely in the pan before slicing and serving.

Maple & Olive Oil Tahini Granola

Makes
3–4 cups

When I'm stressed, I make granola. So in periods of high anxiety, my apartment is filled to the brim with crunchy, lightly sweet, golden clusters of oats, nuts, and seeds. I guess it's not such a bad coping mechanism.

There's something very satisfying about making granola at home. I can't figure out whether it's because it's so easy to make, or because you end up saving some funds by making a fresher and crunchier version than store-bought. Whatever the case, I'm addicted to the instant gratification that homemade granola gives me. Not to mention it's super portable as a snack or even as a gift for someone because it travels well, especially when you throw it into a cute mason jar.

The base of this granola is made with tahini, maple syrup, and a touch of olive oil. These three factors create a rich sweet-and-savory flavor profile and also some pretty intense clusters, which is the primary reason we're eating granola in the first place, right?

⅓ cup tahini

¼ cup maple syrup

2 tablespoons extra-virgin olive oil

1½ cups whole, skin-on, unsalted almonds or mixed nuts of choice, slightly crushed or chopped

¾ cup unsweetened coconut chips

2 cups rolled oats

1 tablespoon hemp seeds

1 tablespoon chia seeds

1 tablespoon flaxseed meal

½ teaspoon kosher salt

½ teaspoon ground cinnamon

Preheat the oven to 325°F and line a baking sheet with parchment paper.

In a medium bowl, combine the tahini, maple syrup, and olive oil, and mix until smooth.

In another medium bowl, combine the nuts, coconut chips, rolled oats, hemp seeds, chia seeds, flaxseed, salt, and cinnamon. Once they're mixed, add these dry ingredients to the tahini-maple syrup mixture. Stir to combine so that the tahini mixture thoroughly coats the nuts, seeds, and oats.

Spoon the granola onto your parchment paper–lined baking sheet. Spread the mixture out so that everything has room to breathe and some personal space—this will ensure an even, crisp bake.

Bake for 30 to 40 minutes, tossing the granola every 10 minutes or so to ensure that everything becomes golden and toasty.

Once you remove the baking sheet from the oven, do not stir the granola! This is how we achieve clusters, so let it sit until it has cooled completely before breaking it apart into clusters. Store in an airtight container or sealed mason jar on your counter or pantry for up to 2 weeks.

Maple
& Olive Oil
Tahini Granola

Rice Crispy
Granola

Cinnamon Pain Perdu
with Almond Butter Caramel

Serves 2

While I was in college, each year when my birthday rolled around (November 18th for all of you who would like to send me almond butter jars or tahini in celebration), I knew where I needed to go for breakfast: La Note on Shattuck Avenue. I was never interested in any of the savory options but instead went straight for the Brioche Pain Perdu. This true state-of-the-art French toast was soaked in an orange flower water batter and sprinkled with confectioners' sugar and lavender honey. Soft, light, but impossibly decadent, the La Note French toast reminds me of a celebration, and so does my own Cinnamon Pain Perdu. You can use brioche here, your leftover French bread from last night, or my personal favorite, sourdough. And don't blame me if you want to carry this Almond Butter Caramel everywhere you go. I do it, too.

Almond Butter Caramel

3 large Medjool dates, pitted

3 tablespoons creamy almond butter

2 tablespoons coconut sugar

½ cup unsweetened vanilla almond milk

French Toast

2 eggs

1 teaspoon vanilla extract

1 teaspoon ground cinnamon

2 tablespoons unsweetened vanilla non-dairy milk

Coconut oil for pan-frying

2 large slices sourdough bread

Coconut sugar for sprinkling

Confectioners' sugar (optional)

Fresh berries (optional)

Prepare the Almond Butter Caramel: In a high-speed blender, combine the dates, almond butter, coconut sugar, and almond milk. Blend until smooth and set aside.

Make the French Toast: In a shallow dish, beat together the eggs, vanilla, cinnamon, and non-dairy milk.

Heat a medium skillet over medium heat. Once the skillet is hot, add coconut oil (I use about ½ tablespoon per slice). Submerge one piece of bread into the egg mixture, flipping to make sure it's evenly soaked. Sprinkle each side of the soaked bread with a bit of coconut sugar and place the bread in the pan. Pan-fry 3 to 5 minutes per side, or until the French toast is cooked through and golden brown on both sides.

Drizzle the Almond Butter Caramel over the slices of French toast and top them with confectioners' sugar and berries, if desired. Serve immediately.

Blueberry Muffin Loaf Cake

Makes 1 loaf,
10—12 slices

Wouldn't it be nice if your bowl of oatmeal and favorite blueberry muffin decided to get together and form one gorgeous breakfast? Or so I caught myself thinking while staring maybe just a little too long at the blueberry muffin behind the glass at my local coffee shop. Once I got my coffee and my act together, I decided to create this blueberry muffin loaf cake situation.

Teaching myself how to bake has been both a blessing and a curse, because the ability to make whatever I want whenever I want is a mildly dangerous skill to have. Another realization I've had about myself, other than my treacherous ability to bake at all hours, is that I have a tendency to turn everything into a loaf. This is my case in point. Muffins are great and all, but that ratio of fluffy middle to crunchy crust in a loaf? It cannot be beat.

¼ cup coconut oil, melted and cooled, plus extra for greasing the pan

1 egg

⅓ cup creamy almond butter

1 teaspoon vanilla extract

2 tablespoons maple syrup

2 tablespoons fresh lemon juice

½ teaspoon grated lemon zest

¾ cup coconut sugar, plus 1 tablespoon for topping

1¼ cups almond flour

1¼ cups oat flour

1½ teaspoons baking powder

¼ teaspoon kosher salt

1 teaspoon ground cinnamon

¼ cup unsweetened almond milk

1 cup fresh blueberries

Preheat the oven to 350°F and grease the bottom and sides of a 9 × 5-inch loaf pan with coconut oil.

In a medium bowl, beat the egg. Then add the almond butter, ¼ cup coconut oil, vanilla, maple syrup, lemon juice, and lemon zest. Mix until smooth. Add the coconut sugar and stir together until everything is well incorporated.

In a separate medium bowl, whisk together the almond flour, oat flour, baking powder, salt, and cinnamon.

Combine the almond butter mixture with the dry ingredients and stir well to incorporate. Add the almond milk to help everything come together. Gently fold in the blueberries.

Transfer the batter to the prepared loaf pan, tapping the pan on the counter and smoothing out the top to make sure it is evenly distributed. Sprinkle the 1 tablespoon coconut sugar on top, and bake for 30 to 35 minutes, until the edges are golden crispy brown and a knife inserted in the center comes out clean.

Once completely cool, run a non-serrated knife alongside the edges of the loaf. Place an upside-down plate on top of the loaf and invert it onto the plate.

RASPBERRY LEMON JOURNEY

Substitute the 1 cup blueberries for 1 cup raspberries and add 1 extra tablespoon of lemon juice and ½ teaspoon extra lemon zest.

Honey-Tahini Scones

Makes
8 scones

2 flax eggs (see Note on page 72)

⅓ cup tahini

5 tablespoons coconut oil, softened until scoopable, plus extra for greasing the baking sheet

¼ cup honey, plus extra (optional) for drizzling

1 teaspoon vanilla extract

1 tablespoon fresh lemon juice

2 tablespoons coconut sugar

2 cups oat flour, plus extra for dusting

¼ teaspoon sea salt

2 teaspoons baking powder

3 tablespoons non-dairy milk (perhaps hemp, almond, or oat)

If I were to conjure up the scones of my dreams, well, you're looking at them right here. They're lightly sweetened with honey and just a tiny touch of coconut sugar. Thanks to the tahini, these are creamy and earthy, and they maintain a stunning crumbly texture that ruins all of your clothing because you won't be able to stop eating them and you'll find crumbs on your sleeves for the rest of the day. Not from personal experience or anything.

I suggest making these with store-bought oat flour because it is finer in texture than the oat flour you can create at home. However, if that's inaccessible, you can most definitely use rolled oats that you've ground into flour in your food processor or blender. Try to get it as fine as possible, but it's no big deal if it's not crazy pulverized because it will give these a really hearty, wholesome, oaty texture.

Prepare the flax eggs and set aside. In a medium bowl, mix together the tahini, coconut oil, and honey. Add the vanilla, lemon juice, and 1 tablespoon of the coconut sugar. Stir to combine.

At this point your flax egg should have thickened up. Add it to the tahini mixture and stir to combine.

Add the oat flour and salt to the tahini mixture. Now, add the baking powder on top, sprinkling it over the entire surface area of the flour and salt. Fold everything together thoroughly. Once you've mixed everything so it's as fully incorporated as it can be, add the non-dairy milk to help pull it all together.

Form the dough into a ball and transfer it to a floured surface. Flatten it into a disk that's about 1½ inches thick. Use a large knife to cut the disk into 8 wedges.

Lightly grease a baking sheet with coconut oil or line it with parchment paper. Transfer the separated wedges to the prepared baking sheet. Sprinkle the tops with the remaining 1 tablespoon coconut sugar.

Place the baking sheet in your refrigerator to chill for at least 15 minutes or as long as 30 minutes.

(*recipe continues*)

Preheat the oven to 400°F.

Once the oven is heated, remove the baking sheet from the fridge and bake the scones for about 15 minutes. The scones should be golden and crisp around the tops and sides.

Remove the baking sheet from the oven and let the scones cool on the baking sheet. Enjoy the scones by themselves or with a drizzle of honey, and especially with your coffee or tea.

WHAT IS
A FLAX EGG?

There is probably nothing that sounds less cute than a "flax egg." But the thing about flax eggs is that they make all the difference for people who can't tolerate eggs or who follow a vegan diet. A flax egg is a combination of water and flaxseed meal (a.k.a. ground-up flaxseed) that yields a thick, gelatinous (are you cringing, because same) substance. When added to recipes in the place of eggs, it works as a binder and a replacement for eggs with a nice little dose of fiber to boot. I actually really love the way flax eggs work in recipes; they make the texture a little denser than eggs would, while allowing the recipe to remain light. And I appreciate the fact that it makes recipes a lot more accessible for different dietary preferences or needs. Here is the formula for a flax egg; it can be substituted in most recipes that call for eggs, but where more than two eggs are called for, I stick with regular eggs, as the recipe may be compromised.

1 tablespoon flaxseed meal +
2½ tablespoons warm water

Let sit for 5 minutes until a gel-like texture is achieved.

Masala Scrambled Eggs

Serves 2–3

5 eggs

½ teaspoon ground turmeric

Freshly ground black pepper

1 tablespoon extra-virgin olive oil

1 medium red onion, diced

½ teaspoon ground cumin

¼ teaspoon cayenne pepper

Kosher salt

Handful of fresh cilantro, stems removed, roughly chopped, plus more for garnish

2 green chiles

Handful fresh spinach, roughly chopped

Toast for serving

This recipe was *the* Sunday breakfast in my house when I was growing up. We'd pair these masala scrambled eggs with some extra-toasted sourdough bread and use the delightfully, and very audibly, crunchy toast (arguably a cracker at this point) to scoop up the eggs, *sans* forks. The utensil simply wasn't necessary.

Turmeric, cayenne, and cumin are all major players here, and along with onions, green chiles, and cilantro, this is a pretty zesty, herby, spicy way to wake up in the morning. It's also a very easy throw-it-together meal to double when you invited guests over for breakfast and sort of forgot they were coming.

In a medium bowl, beat the eggs with ½ teaspoon of the turmeric and a dash of black pepper. Whisk until the eggs are well beaten and frothy and the spices are nicely incorporated. Set the eggs aside.

Heat a medium skillet over medium heat and add the olive oil. Once the oil is shimmering, add the onions to the pan and cook until they become translucent and are a little golden around the edges, 5 to 6 minutes.

Add the cumin, the remaining ¼ teaspoon turmeric, the cayenne, and salt to taste, and cook until the spices smell aromatic and have roasted, darkening slightly in color, about 2 minutes. Add the cilantro and green chiles. Cook for another minute.

Now add the beaten eggs to the onions. Cook, scrambling the eggs until they are completely cooked through. Add the spinach and cook until it wilts, 2 to 3 minutes.

Garnish with cilantro and enjoy with toast!

Spicy Turmeric Quiche

Serves 6

I've never understood quiche. Are you a breakfast item? Are you made for brunch? Are you there as the savory component for an afternoon tea? Literally *what are you?* And then I realized I don't need to put quiche in a corner. Quiche can be whatever it wants to be. And so I made it spicy and added turmeric.

The crust of this quiche is made with a blend of spices, garlic, herbs, and almond meal. I didn't want the crust to just be a place for the filling to live, but rather a star in its own right! As for the filling, I adore the combination of spinach and onions but you're more than welcome to switch it up to your liking. Add some arugula! Maybe some bell peppers! Even some mushrooms! Moral of the story is that quiche is a versatile, excellent thing and I really have to apologize to quiche everywhere for my previous oversights.

Crust

½ cup extra-virgin olive oil, plus extra for greasing the pie dish

2 cups almond meal

2 tablespoons coconut flour

1 teaspoon garlic powder

¼ teaspoon ground cumin

½ teaspoon dried oregano

½ teaspoon kosher salt

½ teaspoon cracked black pepper

¼ teaspoon red pepper flakes

1 tablespoon nutritional yeast

3 tablespoons unsweetened almond milk

Filling

1 tablespoon extra-virgin olive oil

½ white onion, chopped

Kosher salt

1 cup (packed) fresh spinach

5 eggs

½ teaspoon freshly ground black pepper

1 teaspoon ground cumin

¼ teaspoon cayenne pepper

¼ teaspoon ground turmeric

¼ cup unsweetened almond milk

Preheat the oven to 400°F. Grease an 8-inch pie dish with extra-virgin olive oil and set it aside.

Make the crust: In a medium bowl, combine the almond meal, coconut flour, garlic powder, cumin, oregano, salt, black pepper, red pepper flakes, and nutritional yeast. Stir together well. Then add the ½ cup olive oil and almond milk, and mix thoroughly. Press the crust mixture into the pie dish, covering the bottom and up the sides. Bake the crust for 15 to 20 minutes, until the edges are lightly golden.

Prepare the filling: Heat the olive oil in a small skillet over medium heat. Add the onions and a pinch of salt, and sauté until they are translucent, tender, and starting to brown, 5 to 6 minutes. Then add the spinach and cook with the onions until it has wilted. Set the mixture aside to let cool.

In a medium bowl, whisk the eggs with the black pepper, cumin, cayenne, turmeric, and salt (I use ½ teaspoon). Then add the cooled sautéed onions and spinach. Finally, stir in the almond milk.

Pour the filling into the baked crust and bake for 20 to 25 minutes, until a knife or toothpick inserted in the center comes out clean and the crust has darkened in color. The egg filling will have risen but will fall once it cools slightly. Let the quiche cool for about 10 minutes. Then cut it into slices and serve immediately.

Tomato Egg Curry

Serves 3–4

This is a dish to make if you want the glitz and glam of baked eggs in tomato sauce but don't feel like baking eggs in tomato sauce. I was inspired by a traditional Punjabi egg curry, a North Indian dish that is cooked in this way, adding boiled eggs to a punchy tomato-based sauce made with garlic, ginger, onions, and masala. I like leaving the boiled eggs whole and scoring them so that the sauce finds its way in, but you are also welcome to halve them so that the sauce gets *really* all up in there. My mom used to eat this dish as a kid growing up in India, so it always reminds me of her. Note: this transitions beautifully to lunch or dinner, too!

6 eggs

2 tablespoons extra-virgin olive oil

7 fresh curry leaves (omit if you're unable to locate some!)

½ teaspoon mustard seeds

1 yellow onion, diced

3 garlic cloves, halved

½ teaspoon ground turmeric

¼ teaspoon cayenne pepper (or ½ teaspoon if you want it spicier)

1 teaspoon ground cumin

1 (28-ounce) can crushed tomatoes

Kosher salt

Handful of roughly chopped fresh cilantro, plus extra for serving

2 green chiles, stem removed, trimmed, and slit open lengthwise

Toasted bread, rice, or roti for serving

 Bring a medium saucepan of water to a boil. Once the water has come to a rolling boil, lower the eggs into the water one by one, using a slotted spoon. Boil for 8 minutes. Pour the water out of the pot and transfer the eggs to a colander. Transfer the eggs to a bowl of ice water and let them cool in this cute little bath for 2 to 3 minutes to stop them from cooking further.

Peel and score the eggs (make shallow slashes using a paring knife) or cut them in half so when we add them to the masala, the sauce will find its way in. Set the eggs aside.

Heat the olive oil in a deep medium saucepan over medium heat. Once the oil starts to shimmer, add the curry leaves (if using) and the mustard seeds. Cook for a few seconds, until the mustard seeds start to sizzle, then add the onions. Cook the onions for 5 to 7 minutes, or until they become lightly browned. Then, add the garlic.

Cook the onions and the garlic together in the oil until they start to brown around the edges, after 2 to 3 minutes. Now add the turmeric, cayenne, and cumin. Cook and brown the spices for 2 to 3 minutes until fragrant. You can add a splash of water if the mixture starts to burn.

Add the tomatoes, cover the pan, and cook over medium heat for 20 minutes so the masala infuses with the sauce, stirring often. Then season with salt to taste.

Add the handful of cilantro and the green chiles to the sauce. Cook for about 5 more minutes, then add the scored or halved boiled eggs.

Cook on low heat for another 3 to 4 minutes, stirring gently so that the sauce coats the eggs well. Garnish with cilantro, and serve with your favorite toasted bread, rice, or roti.

Caramelized Onion Savory Oatmeal

Serves 1

I really discovered oatmeal in college, where I would get it from the dining hall (thank you for your service, Crossroads dining hall of UC Berkeley), mash half a banana into it, slice the other half into coins to gingerly lay on top, and finish it all off with a huge scoop of peanut butter and a sprinkle of cinnamon. As I matured, my oatmeal creations followed suit. However, it wasn't until recently that I dabbled in the world of savory oatmeal.

Savory oats sort of freaked me out at first, mostly because I am a creature of habit. But this dish has really changed the game for me. It's hearty, comforting, and warming straight down to your soul. Caramelizing the onions allows for a bit of sweetness to come through, which balances out the spices and the earthy, grounding oats. While you could most certainly exercise your freedom of topping rights, I highly recommend the choices here: a crispy fried egg, creamy avocado, and cilantro.

½ cup rolled oats

1 cup vegetable broth

1 tablespoon extra-virgin olive oil, plus extra for the skillet and for drizzling

¼ yellow onion, diced

Kosher salt and freshly ground black pepper to taste

½ teaspoon ground turmeric

½ teaspoon ground cumin

½ cup (packed) fresh arugula

1 egg

½ avocado, sliced

Fresh cilantro leaves or other herbs, roughly chopped, for garnish

In a medium pot, bring your oats and vegetable broth to a boil. Cook, stirring frequently, until the oats become soft, creamy, and have absorbed almost all of the broth.

While the oats are cooking, heat the olive oil in a medium saucepan over medium heat. Once it shimmers, add the onions and sauté until they become tender and start to caramelize, 15 to 20 minutes, reducing to medium-low heat if the onions start to darken too quickly. Season the onions with salt and black pepper.

Add the turmeric and cumin to the onions and roast the spices with the onions for 2 to 3 minutes. The spices should smell fragrant and toasty.

When the oats are mostly cooked but have just a little vegetable broth left to absorb, add them to the onions. Stir to combine.

Stir the arugula into the oats until it wilts. Season to taste with salt and pepper.

In a small skillet, heat a dash of olive oil. When it shimmers, crack the egg into the pan and fry until it is done to your liking.

Transfer the oatmeal to a shallow bowl, top it with the fried egg, and add the sliced avocado. Drizzle a bit of olive oil on top and add some freshly ground black pepper and salt. Garnish with cilantro or fresh herbs of your choosing.

Morning Soft-Serve

Serves 1

I know myself well enough to know that I mostly go for a sweet breakfast over a savory one. This Morning Soft-Serve is mostly to blame for this life choice. It's hard to go back to simple eggs after starting my day with something reminiscent of dessert.

I like to pretend that I am Picasso with this breakfast soft-serve, using the base ingredients you see below as a blank canvas for adding whatever toppings I please. Some of my favorites are berries, granola, nuts, or more almond/peanut butter (always).

It's incredible how this gives me Frosty vibes (if you know, you know), yet is just made with a base of frozen bananas. So, the next time you find yourself with many bananas that have all decided to ripen at the same time, it's a good move to freeze a few to make this for breakfast and bake banana bread with the rest.

2 frozen bananas (see Note on page 60)

1 heaping tablespoon crunchy almond butter or peanut butter

1 tablespoon hemp seeds

½ teaspoon ground cinnamon

5 tablespoons unsweetened vanilla non-dairy milk

Toppings of choice

In a food processor or high-speed blender, combine the bananas, nut butter, hemp seeds, and cinnamon. Add the non-dairy milk and pulse to blend. It will seem like it's not blending easily, and that's okay. You can add a couple more tablespoons of the milk, but know that adding too much liquid will compromise the thick soft-serve consistency we want, so I recommend using a utensil to scrape down the sides of your processor or blender and keep blending until smooth.

Transfer the soft-serve to a bowl and serve it immediately with your toppings of choice.